£3.99

CONTENTS

Written by Michael Heatley.

Layout and design by Louise Ivimy and Nigel Money.

Published by
GRANDREAMS LIMITED
Jadwin House, 205/211 Kentish Town Road,
London, NW5 2JU

Printed in Italy.

ISBN 1 85830 0614

All information correct at time of going to press.

JOHN AND ULRIKA

They couldn't be more different - the tall, dark, handsome sportsman and the bubbly blonde TV presenter. Yet this pair of opposites certainly attracts - over eleven million viewers at the last count, with just a little help from their well-muscled friends.

Stockholm-born Ulrika needs no introduction. Since becoming a household name as Breakfast TV's favourite weather girl, the outgoing 25-year-old has presented TV-am's careers advice line, co-presented the current affairs programme *6 O'Clock Live* and fronted her own summer programme *Ulrika On The Move*. Now she's moved to the most compelling TV spectacle around, helping contenders through their triumphs and disasters to the delight of the arena audience at Birmingham's National Indoor Arena - and of course, the millions watching at home.

Though she insists she's no fitness freak, Ulrika admits to numbering tennis, basketball, horseriding and volleyball among the ways she lets off steam. But she won't take things too far, as she showed when she was presenting Hang Tough around 15 feet off the ground. "The audience shouted 'jump', but I was under strict instructions not to put my safety at risk," explained the girl who succeeded Anneka Rice as 'Rear of the Year', "so I climbed down the ladder and everyone booed and hissed!"

Nevertheless, presenting *Gladiators* has inspired her to join a gym and "become a fitter person all round." And that, says Ulrika, is what *Gladiators* is all about. "They make you believe that with enough hard work it's possible to achieve the body you want."

John Fashanu, Premier League footballer and captain of Wimbledon FC, has already made a name for himself on the small screen, presenting BBC2's *On The Line*, BBC1's *Good Sport*, and Channel 4's *Seven Sport*, as well as making a guest appearance on *A Question of Sport*. Also off the pitch, John works to help the aged and has been honoured for his work against apartheid. With business interests of his own to look after too, it's a wonder he can fit *Gladiators* into his busy schedule.

John has little to prove in the fitness stakes. In the last ten years, apart from winning an FA Cup medal and leading his goalscorers for six seasons running, John has supplemented the soccer skills that took him into the England team with Tai-Chi and Wing Chung Kung Fu. Yet he's not had the chance to challenge the Gladiators himself yet. "I can see myself in a lot of the contenders," he admits. "I've tried some challenges on my own, but without being tackled by a Gladiator. I hope one day I'll have chance to do it properly." Maybe team-mate Vinny Jones will come along too...Psycho versus Warrior - now that would be worth seeing!

Meanwhile, 30-year-old John is happy to enjoy a ringside seat as the bone-crunching contender-versus-Gladiator confrontations thrill the eleven million plus audiences. A new series is scheduled for the autumn of 1993, but there'll be live events meanwhile, so stay tuned - and keep your *Gladiators Fact File* close at hand for the latest in facts and info on the human sculptures they call the Gladiators.

Cobra's Champion Diet

Breakfast: Porridge, four poached eggs on toast, cup of tea
Lunch: Jacket potato with tuna and salad or large cheese and tomato pizza
Between meals: Bananas and ten egg whites
Dinner: Large bowl of pasta with tuna, washed down with a litre of orange juice

COBRA

> **"Self confidence and determination are vital qualities if you want to be a contender. You must have speed and agility, strength and power. It's mentally tough."**

Super-fit Cobra is the Gladiator who Hangs Toughest. They call him King of the Rings, and you'd better believe it! But he nearly didn't make it onto the team at all, having originally applied to be a contestant. "I'd heard on the radio they were looking for people," he explains, "but I thought all the Gladiators had been hired. Then they phoned me up and said I was too big to be a contender - and why not audition for the part of a Gladiator?"

After the very toughest of fitness tests, including a duel to the death with Hawk, he made it through to become one of the elite - and he was so impressive on the rings that he was immediately marked out as top Gladiator on that particular challenge. He's pretty fast on The Wall too!

"The secret of success in Hanging Tough," says Cobra, "is to relax completely and let yourself hang. I do a fair amount of stretching, so I think that helped."

Cobra's high kicks as he enters the Gladiatorial arena mark him out as a man with plenty of confidence. That confidence is born of a punishing gym routine that he does every day: chest, triceps and shoulders first, then legs, back and biceps. You only need to look at the pictures to see the results.

COBRA - AT-A-GLANCE

Height: 6 feet (1m 83cm)
Weight: 16 stone (102kg)
Day job: Engineer for a large Japanese company
Sports: Bodybuilding and martial arts (including full contact karate)

"I do a lot of cross training, including circuit training which involves aerobic fitness and weights. Twice a week I go running for two miles...it's really good for building stamina."

FLAME - AT-A-GLANCE

Height:	6 feet (1m 83cm)
Weight:	10 stone (64kg)
Vital Statistics:	35-25-35
Honours:	Oregon State Championship swimming finalist
Sports:	Track and field athletics, swimming

FLAME

If anyone ever claims Gladiators are all muscle and no brains, then Flame is just the person to illuminate them. She arrived in Britain six years ago with a degree in business administration - having spent six months at Edinburgh University on a student exchange, she liked it so much she came back to stay!

Flame is the only current Gladiator who has never been a dedicated bodybuilder, but this is no disadvantage when it comes to chasing contenders in the Atlaspheres, which she does with great speed and power. While U.S. Gladiators are heavily muscled, Flame is comparatively slight. Like the field and track champion she is, Flame prefers the challenges where speed and agility count for the most - though she's been known to get pretty riled when a pugil stick is put into her hand, and at six foot she has a pretty enviable reach!

Despite her sensational figure, Oregon-born Flame is no pushover when it comes to Gladiating, as many a female contender has found to her cost.

Flame's Figure Diet

Flame looks after her superb figure by limiting herself to 3,000 calories a day in a high carbohydrate, energy-giving diet. Porridge, jacket potatoes, pasta, spinach and broccoli may not sound the most appetising food in the world, but it seems to have done wonders for Flame. "The healthier I eat," she says, "the more conscious I am of feeling good." And looking good!

COBRA
FLAME
HAWK
JET
LIGHTNING
PANTHER
PHOENIX
SARACEN
SCORPIO
SHADOW
WARRIOR
WOLF

HAWK

> "Doing something as physical as *Gladiators* after being a bodybuilder for so long is great. There's a real feeling of camaraderie on the show."

He got his name from the *Gladiators* crew because of the way he swoops on his prey - but Cardiff-born Hawk has the muscle to match his undoubted agility. "I started training ten years ago, mainly for athletics," he says. "But when I started weight training, I found it just took over."

Since then he's pursued a rigorous training programme that's built him up into a Gladiator to be feared. But preparation can be as much mental as physical, and Hawk admits that sometimes relaxation is as important as exercise.

Hawk's strict diet includes 18 egg whites a day as well as tuna, salmon and white meat - all washed down with skimmed milk and protein drinks.

Hawk's all-round sporting skills make him the Gladiator who can - and does - tackle everything. The determination in his eyes speaks volumes, and tells you that here's one Gladiator who thinks the show is more than just a series of games.

Hawk Hangs Tough

Hawk's training schedule has changed in the last two years as he's added agility and fitness to his superbly muscled body. He now only weight trains four days a week, using shuttle runs, wall climbing and hanging from bars at up to 15 minutes at a stretch to give him the flexibility and agility that make him a Gladiator to be feared.

HAWK - AT-A-GLANCE

Height: 6ft 1in (185cm)
Weight: 17 stone (108kg)
Honours: Mr Wales title (winner twice), long jumped for Cardiff
Sports: Rugby, boxing, archery, long jump

JET - AT-A-GLANCE

Height:	5ft 7in (170cm)
Weight:	10 stone (63kg)
Vital statistics:	38-25-35
Honours:	British Gymnastics Squad
Sports:	Dance, gymnastics, hill walking

JET

"When they announce your name you think, 'I can either stand here and freeze, or I can go for it!' Competing gives you a buzz."

A crackshot in Danger-Zone, her specialist challenge, Jet's eagle eyes are just one part of a potent package! Having studied dance as well as gymnastics, Jet is both perfectly proportioned and superbly balanced. Her other favourite event is Hang-Tough. "It gives you a wonderful feeling of adrenaline," she says.

Like Scorpio, Jet has appeared on film in *Anna Ballerina* and *She Wolf Of London*. But it's her small screen appearances that have made Jet a big name - and one thing she's never lacked is confidence. "I had done quite a lot of TV work before, so I felt comfortable in front of the cameras." If anything she can sometimes be too eager, and in the first series once had to restart The Wall after pursuing her contender too fiercely and falling off.

Jet has been a sports and fitness enthusiast since she was just six. Now 22, she says owning a dance and fitness club is her long term ambition. A stint in pantomime in *Jack and the Beanstalk* proves that Jet (real name Diane Youdale) is more than just some body. And as a Gladiator she's already reached the top of the tree...

Jet Jogs To Success

To keep her sleek figure, Jet updates her fitness programme regularly, varying her routines every four to six weeks: "My body is extremely responsive to exercise." She does a lot of hill running on the North Downs near her home to build stamina, and has her own stairmaster to keep her fit at home.

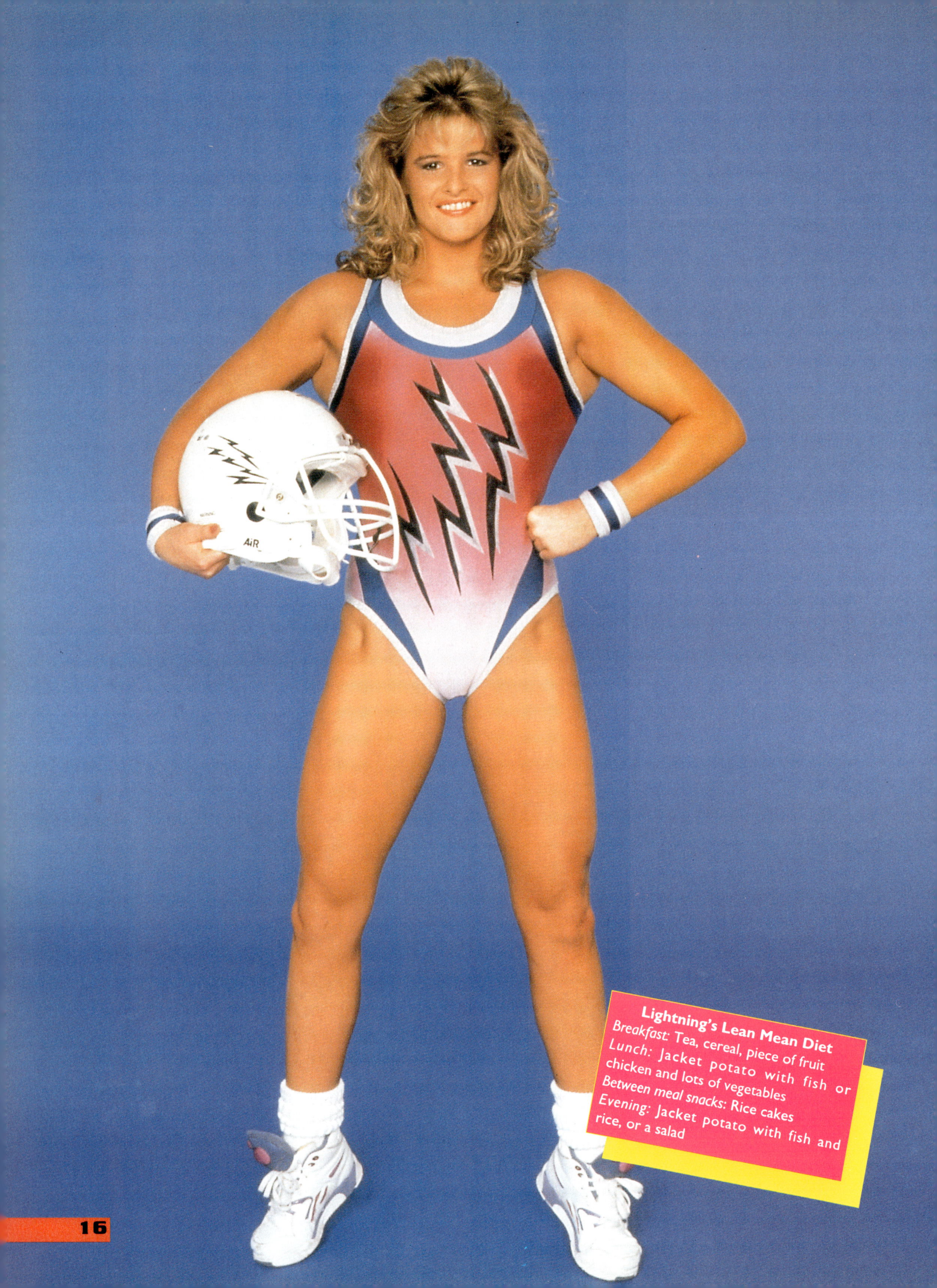

Lightning's Lean Mean Diet

Breakfast: Tea, cereal, piece of fruit
Lunch: Jacket potato with fish or chicken and lots of vegetables
Between meal snacks: Rice cakes
Evening: Jacket potato with fish and rice, or a salad

LIGHTNING

> **"Being a Gladiator is about major determination and a bit of aggression... you've got to have that to succeed."**

Together with Cobra, Lightning was the last Gladiator to join, having applied to be a contender. And the qualities the producers saw in her are obvious. A gymnast since the tender age of six, she's competed all over Europe and won no fewer than 32 medals! That early dedication proved to be her passport to *Gladiators*, and the fame and fortune that's followed.

"My father used to be a wrestler," she explains of her life-long quest for physical fitness - and she still trains with him, not to mention doing an hour of step aerobics, a half-hour bike ride and a long walk. She was an aerobics and weight training instructor, but found she was spending too much time training others and not enough on her own body! Now she's more than made up for lost time.

The challenges Lightning most relishes are the Atlaspheres and Hang Tough where her gym workouts really come into their own. She's also a dab hand at the Duel, but explains, "you have to control those sticks and I only have small hands. You need a lot of practice..."

LIGHTNING - AT-A-GLANCE

Height:	5ft 7in (170cm)
Weight:	9st 5lb (59kg)
Vital statistics:	38-26-35
Honours:	Former bodybuilding champion, British athletics squad, runner-up British Bodybuilding Championship
Sports:	Swimming, gymnastics, aerobics, weight training

COBRA
FLAME
HAWK
JET
LIGHTNING
PANTHER
PHOENIX
SARACEN
SCORPIO
SHADOW
WARRIOR
WOLF

PANTHER - AT-A-GLANCE

Height:	5ft 7in (170cm)
Weight:	9st 7lb (60kg)
Vital statistics:	36-24-36
Honours:	Miss Great Britain, Miss Europe, Miss World, Miss Universe, Miss Central Britain and Miss Russia amateur bodybuilding titles

PANTHER

> **"I think it would be quite nice if the British Gladiators could have a go at the Americans. It's what everyone wants!"**

Panther's strength on the Duel gave one contender cause to complain that, "she never gave me the time to attack". Panther more than lives up to her name as a predatory feline who just loves to get her claws into contenders. Yet her favourite challenge is Atlaspheres. "I'm quite fast and once my adrenaline started pumping I couldn't wait to roll down those platforms and crash into the others." A shoulder injury in the first series kept her out of the Duel on occasions, but she'll be looking to get back on the podium next time round.

As her long list of titles suggests, Panther (real name Helen Madderson) is a super-fit woman who just happens to be the most successful female amateur bodybuilder of all time. "I'm the biggest girl Gladiator, too," she boasts.

The *Gladiators* production team spotted Panther on the Noel Edmonds Show and asked her to audition. Now the Newcastle-born Gladiator has been part of the competition to *Noel's House Party*. Back at home in the north-east, Panther runs her own gym and leisurewear company.

Panther Goes Stateside

At least three times a year, the exclusive Gold's Gym at Venice Beach, California, plays host to Panther, on the prowl for hints to use at her own Work-out World in Northumberland. "Everywhere I looked I could see a famous bodybuilder," she says of her American experience.

COBRA
FLAME
HAWK
JET
LIGHTNING
PANTHER
PHOENIX
SARACEN
SCORPIO
SHADOW
WARRIOR
WOLF

"I'm a tough cookie and I think if I was attacked I'd stand a pretty good chance of defending myself."

PHOENIX - AT-A-GLANCE

Height:	5ft 8in (173cm)
Vital statistics:	35-23-33
Honours:	Miss Midlands 1990-92, Miss Oscars 1991 WABBA Midlands Figure (bodybuilding), Miss UK 1990-91
Sports:	Thai boxing, kick boxing

PHOENIX

Believe it or not, Phoenix started bodybuilding to tone herself up after having a baby - and eight months later was crowned Miss UK. "I knew the other girls had been training a lot longer than I had," she admits, "but I was confident."

If it sounds like she's singing her own praises, then you're not far wrong! Away from the Gladiatorial arena, Phoenix is a budding singer and songwriter, and has already released a single. But all that must fit in with a schedule that, in the bodybuilding season, sees her train three hours a day and follow a low fat, high carbohydrate, high protein diet.

Central television featured Phoenix in a documentary that highlighted the feminine side of bodybuilding, and she's certainly a a great advertisement for the sport. Yet her competitive days have had to come to a close - temporarily, at least - with the demands of the series. "I haven't got time to do competitions any more," she says, "because it takes a lot of commitment and dedication to be a Gladiator." And Phoenix should know.

Phoenix Passes The Test

Phoenix had to undergo the strictest of gym tests at Woolwich, south-east London devised by Olympic standard coaches John Anderson and Tom McNab that encompassed almost every challenge included in the programme. Her stamina and agility proved she was up to the punishing standard required, and so joined the four other original female Gladiators (ex-contender Lightning joined later) as one of the elite.

"Every programme is the same for us. If we don't do well on one show we know we'll be back next time. But the contenders only have one chance to make the best of it."

Saracen's Screen Test

Saracen has been on screen twice before...when he was still plain Mike Lewis! He worked part-time at a London gym populated by celebrities, and the cameras were often there. "They showed me on TV, and I didn't know about it until someone told me the next day." Then he made a two-minute live appearance on the ITV Telethon, in which he was interviewed by Emma Freud - since then the sky's been the limit!

SARACEN

Born plain Mike Lewis, Saracen took time to get known in his own right. He's even portrayed heavyweight boxer Frank Bruno in a TV programme - tribute in itself to his physique. Now, though, he's recognised everywhere - even in Tesco's when he goes shopping with his girlfriend Chrissie Mullings, one of the first series contenders.

Saracen is a specialist on The Wall, and has a phenomenal success rate when it comes to catching and unsticking opponents with his unique blend of speed and strength. "A couple got away," he grumbled, but sportingly admits, "that shows how good they were."

But his favourite is Hang Tough, for which he has the upper body strength to excel. "You have to time it just right," he explains of the shifts in direction that so often wrong-footed (or should that be wrong-handed?) his bemused opponents.

Saracen worked in a central London gym before becoming a fireman, having taken up weight training at the age of 19 while in the catering trade. "I had three hours to kill between 3pm and 6pm," he explained. "There was no time to go home and come back again, so I started training."

A skinny, eleven and a half stone weakling soon filled out to become the superb physical specimen that Saracen is today.

SARACEN - AT-A-GLANCE

Height:	6ft 4in (193cm)	*Day job:*	Fireman
Weight:	17 stone (108kg)	*Sports:*	Weight training and aerobics

"People seem to have taken the show to their hearts. We were happily surprised at how much it took off. It's been a wonderful experience."

Scorpio At School

An appetite for physical fitness was only one of the things Scorpio picked up during her education. The others? Several O levels, an A level and honours from London's prestigious Guildhall School of Drama. Scorpio's advice? Keep up the schoolwork - something she'll definitely be passing on to her two-year-old daughter.

SCORPIO

Born in the Isle of Man, statuesque Scorpio is a very singular Gladiator indeed. This undisputed megastar of our TV screens rates movie stars as her biggest influences. Yet Scorpio was always one step ahead of her idols. "I read *Conan The Barbarian* when I was about 14, before the film had even been made," she says.

You might have guessed that Scorpio is an Arnold Schwarzenegger fan. And maybe he's a fan of hers, since the attractive ex-model has made film appearances of her own in the *Meaning of Life, Mountains On The Moon* and Robbie Coltrane's hilarious *Nuns On The Run* to name just three. She's also starred in a video with man-mountain Meatloaf - somebody few females could measure up against!

She's proved a great success on The Wall. "The second time," she says with justifiable pride, "I did it faster than the guy who taught us to climb it!"

Scorpio's modelling career started at age 14, but stopped her weight training because she thought having muscles might put people off. But producers saw her photograph in a bodybuilding magazine, invited her to audition, and the rest, as they say, is history. "What I'm trying to do is build up my size. I'm training really hard and next time round I'll be a lot bigger and have more cut and definition."

And what Scorpio wants, she gets. "I'm very determined, very fixed and focussed," she insists. But her ultimate aim is to get into science fiction movies with heroes Klaus Kinski, Rutger Hauer - oh, and Arnie naturally!

***SCORPIO* - AT-A-GLANCE**

Height:	5ft 9in (175cm)
Vital Statistics:	38-23-36
Honours:	Inter-school high jump champion (three years running), Miss Isle of Man
Sports:	Gymnastics, horseriding

"There's no escape from me. Contenders had better watch it, because I'm the true test!"

SHADOW - AT-A-GLANCE

Height:	6ft 4in (193cm)
Weight:	19 stone (121kg)
Honours:	1978-80 Mr Teenage Britain, 1982 Novice Mr Britain, 1989 British weightlifting team, second place
Sports:	Bodybuilding, American football, track and field (shot putt, discus, javelin, relay)
Diet:	Chicken, vegetables, potatoes, ice cream, vitamin and mineral supplements

SHADOW

Team leader of the Gladiators, super Shadow has built himself up from a 12 stone weakling to the imposing specimen he is today, thanks to 15 years of training. His daily two hour work-out regime, and his special diet (see panel), have put on the pounds and muscle to equip him for any *Gladiators* event.

One of Shadow's main techniques is to intimidate any contender who dares to put him to the test. "My eyes are looking straight through you and I'm ready to do damage," he tells people - and who's going to argue? It isn't just contenders he damages - several Atlaspheres have felt the heat of the blowtorch after Shadow's aggression had proved just too much.

His audition for *Gladiators* took place at the army barracks in Woolwich, south-east London, where the famed assault course proved no match for his muscle. "I hadn't climbed a rope since high school," he admitted later, "but I just went up there with brute strength."

Few contenders have survived Shadow and lived to tell the tale. One of the few who did, first series winner Weininger Irwin, paid him the ultimate compliment. "For once I would just like the chance to hit him, but he's so quick I never get the chance." Even so, Weininger made UK *Gladiators* history by becoming the first contender to go the distance in the Duel with Shadow.

"The first time Shadow is knocked off," says series producer Nigel Lythgoe, "the place will erupt. But," he adds quickly, "it's gonna take one hell of a person to do it!"

Shadow's Fitness Regime

MORNING: Sessions on the exercise bike and running machine, plus aerobics!

AFTERNOON: routines that increase size and muscle strength.

EVENING: No exercise, but a meal of up to ten chicken breasts, plus rice and veg.

"I would like to get a major movie break. I've been doing a lot of martial arts, so I'm sure that would come in useful. Apart from Arnold and Lundgren, there aren't many skilled big guys on the screen and I'd like to change that."

WARRIOR

With a name like Warrior, you have to be able to compete with the best, and there's no doubting that Warrior more than fits the bill.

Merseyside-born Warrior has enjoyed a globe-trotting lifestyle before coming to the Gladiators arena. After trying out for the England rugby team he spent three years in South Africa before returning to England and building his body from 16 stones to the shape it is in today.

He got the call to join the Gladiators after appearing in a magazine - and since then he has never looked back. Only one regret - bodybuilding has had to take a backseat. "I don't think you can run around and look good at 22 stones," he shrugs.

He's ready, willing and able to tackle any event, but reckons the Atlaspheres are his best challenge. On the Duel Warrior has been known to lose his cool, but who could blame him? After all it's tough balancing his massive 22 stones on so small a platform. In future series, he'd "like to see contenders with a bit more size," since more physical contact would "suit him down to the ground." Gulp!

Warrior's massive intake of up to 10,000 calories daily ensures he's going to remain the heavyweight Gladiator for some while to come.

Wounded Warrior

In Heat 6 of the last series, Warrior damaged his leg in the bone-crunching Atlaspheres, but bravely took part in Danger-Zone with his left leg in plaster from ankle to thigh. He took out losing finalist Kym with a direct hit - where else but in the leg!

WARRIOR - AT-A-GLANCE

Height: 6ft 5in (196cm)
Weight: 21 stone 4lb (135kg)
Honours: Junior British Decathlon champion, Natwest Bank British bodybuilding champion, runner-up Mr Britain
Sports: Rugby (League and Union), decathlon running

"Everyone loves the baddie. People come up to me in the street and say: 'You're the nasty one!' But they know I'm only play acting."

Wolf's Work-out Tips

Training consists of one hour five days a week, plus aerobics every day to speed up his metabolism. An important tip he recommends is to use an exercise bike first thing in the morning before breakfast - something that will speed up your metabolism for the whole day. Wolf spreads his food intake over five or six small meals a day, totalling some 5,000 calories.

WOLF

He may be the smallest male Gladiator bulk wise, but one glimpse of the Wolf is usually enough to strike terror into even the most confident contender. This man doesn't take defeat lying down. Last year's runner-up Kym Dalton beat Wolf on The Wall - and found he was a very bad loser indeed!

Danger-Zone crackshot Wolf enjoys picking his enemies off at will with the rapid-fire air-powered gun, and very rarely gets 'hung up' by a successful contender, though he modestly claims "there's not a lot of skill involved". Tell that to his black and blue victims!

Wolf is among the most distinctive of the Gladiators and admits that being recognised wherever he goes gives him a buzz.

The *Gladiators* wolfman is a real crowd pleaser - to see him leading the NIA thousands in his theme tune *Wild Thing*, is a sight few will forget, almost as awe-inspiring as facing him in combat! And he's going to get more awesome still next series, when Wolf aims to build up another two stones of solid muscle. Since he owns his own gym in Kent, he's got all the facilities he needs.

Wolf, who's made countless appearances in TV commercials and shows like *Perfect Scoundrels*, the *Bobby Davro Show* and *London's Burning* (funnily enough, as a gym owner!) sees his future in *Gladiators*, but also in films. "I would definitely enjoy being in the movies playing the man you love to hate!"

WOLF - AT-A-GLANCE

Height: 6 foot (183cm)
Weight: 15 stone (95kg)
Sports: Kickboxing, snowboarding, rollerblade skating

ATLASPHERES

At first glance, Atlaspheres are a kind of futuristic human dodgems, the kind of thing you'd expect *Star Wars'* Hans Solo to be sentenced to by a sadistic captor. Yes, this is one heck of a challenge to open with - remember those cages are solid steel, and you need protective clothes before you can even *think* of entering. In last year's Heat 6, Warrior fell over inside his Atlasphere after a clash with contender Dean Jackson, and he sustained a severe leg injury.

The object is to use your lower body strength to direct your seven foot diameter Atlasphere over one of the four scoring pods, after you get a head start rolling down the ramps. Pinpointing the sensor in the centre of the pod will release a tell-tale plume of carbon dioxide into the air and you earn three priceless points. The only problem is keeping out of the way of your opponents - one equally determined contender and two musclebound Gladiators!

The sensation - not to mention the heat - is something like being trapped inside a giant tumble dryer, and the objective is not to get *too* creased, particularly with six more strength sapping challenges still to come. The idea is to use the sphere as a running machine, to stand upright and just *run*. "Try to keep moving and don't stand still," advises presenter Ulrika Jonsson. "Try to avoid being cornered, because then you have little chance of moving around." Sounds easy? It isn't!

Warrior is the Gladiator most feared when the wheels of steel start rolling - and with good reason! Strength, endurance and agility are all at a premium on this event - plus the ability to stay calm in a crisis as crashes, collisions and chaos rule!

Top of the female rollerball warriors is Panther, the only Gladiator not to suffer an injury in the event during the first series. "I tended to keep myself low and use very big strides and I think that helped," she reveals. So with strength, strategy and a little bit of luck, contenders can survive the Atlasphere ordeal!

THE WALL

The Wall is an event that gets the adrenaline flowing like no other!

Scaling that daunting, 36 foot high wall and successfully reaching the summit earns a generous ten points, while merely remaining attached after the 60 seconds allotted, brings a hard earned five. As if that wasn't a hard enough test, two Gladiators are on their marks at the bottom (one for each contender) ready to give chase after ten seconds (15 for the women) and more often than not they catch the climbers!

Confidence and arm strength are major factors here. Above all, if you're a contender you have to keep your nerve and avoid being psyched out by a shrewd customer like Cobra. "I chased a contender up The Wall and shouted out, "I'm gonna get you!" he recalls. "He slipped!"

Even Cobra has to admit The Wall is tough on biceps and tendons - but one female contender gave her the slip - literally! She used moisturiser on her legs, which made her too slippery to get hold of. Flame and Scorpio reckon they're more than a match for the high climbers among the female contenders - that is if they don't slip through their fingers!

If contenders can conquer the fear factor, then they're half way to beating the challenge of The Wall. Even Shadow, normally the most fearless of Gladiators, admits to a twinge or two. "I think it's pretty scary," he says. "When you reach a certain height The Wall comes out to meet you, so to try and get past a certain part you're actually leaning backwards and you feel like you're going to fall off."

If Shadow can get the jitters without anyone on his tail, just imagine what an ordeal The Wall is for contenders...

"The first thing I saw when I arrived was The Wall. I thought 'oh no, what *have* I let myself in for?'"

1992 contender

DANGER-ZONE

No other *Gladiators* event demands the same array of skills from its competitors. Contenders not only have to dodge the rain of tennis balls homing in on them from the eagle-eyed Gladiators, they also have to fire accurately at the target from the four weapons stations - which are timed to self-destruct in just ten seconds!

If they score a direct hit on the bullseye, then ten points are theirs and the Gladiator is hung up. But even if they are unsuccessful with the Crossbow, the Bazooka, the Mortar and the Rocket Launcher, contenders can still turn defeat into victory by running through the see-through perspex cylinder and punching the target - providing of course, they stay well clear of the tennis ball barrage.

The Crossbow is furthest from the target, but unlike the others isn't air driven and so gives the best chance of control. But as Wolf points out,

the Gladiators' job isn't that easy either. "That gun gets stuck quite a lot," he says. "There's a lot of luck involved. You don't know whether to shoot left or right - you can only shoot in both directions and hope it works!"

Tennis balls don't sound too threatening...but such is the speed they travel from the Gladiator's compressed air gun - something like a Boris Becker serve - the eye protectors, knee and shoulder pads and body

"This is a game of luck more than skill. You never know whether to shoot left or right."
Wolf

armour are far more than just optional extras. The flashing lights make those projectiles difficult to pick out, so the message to contenders is just keep on running!

Contenders are best advised to dive head-first at the weapons stations, curling themselves into a ball and rolling parachute style to minimise the target for the Gladiators to aim at. Another tactic used against hotshot Gladiator Saracen in last year's series is to persuade him to use up all his ammunition by zig-zagging around the weapon. The Gladiators have 24 balls in their rapid-fire gun - and aim to make every shot count. "Once they've used them," says director Nigel Lythgoe, "contenders can run around without being fired at."

SWINGSHOT

The fourth of the *Gladiators* challenges is so tough that even international football and *Gladiators* host John Fashanu admits he's seen some frightening collisions take place. "It requires endurance and stamina," he explains. "Even then, who knows where the shock cord will drop you?"

Swingshot pits two contenders against two Gladiators simultaneously. The elasticated cord to which contenders and Gladiators are separately hitched enables them to jump down from the elevated platform to the floor, then spring up to grab a ball from one of three differently coloured segments of a central cylinder.

The higher you bounce, the greater number of points you score - providing, that is, you can get the ball back to a pod on top of your home platform. The Gladiators, meanwhile, are hell bent on stopping you, your opponent is swinging in front of you trying to get their own prize, and dropped balls earn you absolutely zilch! .

Even last year's champion contender, Weininger Irwin found the Swingshot experience difficult, "especially returning from the middle to climb up the platform and put the balls in the basket". This strength sapping, energy exhausting spectacle sorts the men from the boys and the girls from the women. No-one who lacks a head for heights need bother applying!

The shock cords are individually adjusted to a contender's weight, allowing them to get maximum spring as they hit the NIA floor and try to soar upwards. But with three events already complete, every last ounce of energy is needed to scale those heights. And many an exhausted contender has got themselves into a tangle after a bone-

crunching collision with all three of his or her rivals.

"Throwing yourself into space can be scary," says Ulrika Jonsson, who's been up there having a last minute word with contenders preparing to do just that. Imagine combining a bungee jump with an Olympic-standard basketball match and you get the picture - little wonder Swingshot is a challenge to be feared!

HANG-TOUGH

With Hang-Tough, you're looking at a game of chess - but this one's played 12 feet above ground level on sixty metal rings hanging four feet apart! To Hang-Tough, a contender has to remain off the mat for a full 60 seconds, repelling the attempts of the opposing Gladiator to make them fall. But that in itself earns only aching muscles. If he or she Hangs-Tough inside the scoring zone (blue coloured rings), contenders add five precious points to their tally. But to make it over to the platform the Gladiator started from, some 50 aching feet away from his or her own point of departure, takes the jackpot with a maximum ten points.

Certain Gladiators don't enjoy Hanging-Tough, as sheer body weight can be a real disadvantage. Cobra, who is undoubtedly one of the Kings of the Rings, has perhaps the perfect proportion of muscle to bulk. He took to it like a fish to water: "I find it the easiest of all the challenges because I have good upper body strength."

Of the female Gladiators, Jet is clearly the one to watch on this challenge. "You can calculate and plot your route," she explains, playing it clever, and proving that brains as well as brute strength are among a Gladiator's keenest assets when it comes to clobbering contenders.

Hang-Tough has already claimed a Gladiator in rehearsal, when Wolf wrenched his finger. Since then he has had to give the game a miss, but don't be surprised to see him giving a top performance next time round.

Only one of the first series contenders managed to make it to the Gladiator's platform in Hang-Tough - ex-karate instructor finalist Kym Dalton, who came within seconds of repeating the feat in the final itself. It takes a special kind of contender to succeed in Hang-Tough...perhaps the most demanding challenge of them all.

DUEL

This is an event that brings out the inner demons in contenders and Gladiators alike. Warrior, who deputised for the injured specialist Shadow in Heat 6, was so enraged by contender Tony Bayford resisting his blows, that he swept him dismissively from the podium with his hands.

The pugil sticks - seven feet of overgrown cotton bud, as one commentator put it - can land a mean blow in the capable hands of a Gladiator. Many a contender has been glad of the standard issue helmet they have been given before taking to the podium.

These platforms are ten feet off the ground and four feet in diameter: there's just 16 inches between the contender and Gladiator, but those 16 inches must not be crossed, as Warrior found to his cost.

The 30 seconds they need to hang on can seem like an eternity to contenders, but survival will bring five invaluable points, or half a second when viewed in Eliminator terms. And that can make quite a difference to the end result.

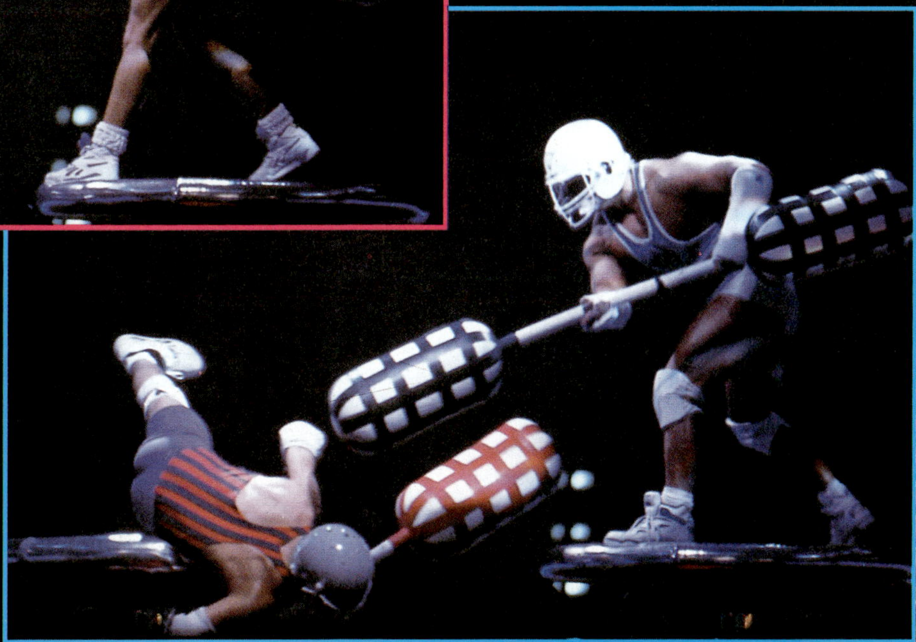

The one-to-one combat of the Duel certainly fires up the Gladiators, if Cobra is any judge. "If we get knocked off it doesn't make us look good...we've got a bit of pride involved. After all," he continues, "who wants to look a laughing stock in front of millions of people?" On the other hand, contenders are giving away several stone to the Gladiator on the other platform just inches away, so the best form of defence is quite often attack. If you can make your opponent lose their balance, their weight will count against them. Strength alone is no guarantee - you need skill to match.

Shadow is the expert, so let's give him the last word: "I don't mess about with that stick. I always tell contenders there's 600 ways to go down," he laughs. "It's the ultimate challenge." Enough said!

ELIMINATOR

Eliminator is the one challenge where the contenders don't have to look over their shoulder for a Gladiator in hot pursuit! Yet the name speaks for itself - there can be only one winner. And it is the contender who comes into this seventh and last challenge with the most points who stands the best chance of eliminating their rival.

Each point gained in excess of their opponent is translated into half a second's

ladder for the women - requires immense body strength (falling off incurs a punishing ten second penalty, while a rolling beam tests co-ordination to the limit. The scramble into the second cargo net - 24 feet this one - takes its toll on aching muscles.

A 90 feet zipline (don't forget to keep your legs up!) takes the competitor down from an aerial platform with a jolt to the travelator - "definitely the hardest part,"

"I think Eliminator is a very good physical challenge. The hardest part is the travelator. If contenders were fresh I'm sure they could do it, but it's a very tough final hurdle."
John Anderson, Olympic coach

lead. The first whistle is for the leading contender, the second for the second placed - who will be looking to eat into the leader's head start.

Many a lost cause has turned into a winning lead as two exhausted contenders attempt to negotiate a course that makes the *Krypton Factor* look like a nursery game! A 20 foot high cargo net is the first obstacle to be surmounted, after which a slide takes you to a scramble sheet. The hand bike - or

presenter John Fashanu reckons. "By then you're tired, your legs have gone, you can see the finish and yet it goes on for miles and miles."

At the last hurdle, the near-exhausted contenders do a Tarzan style swing through the paperburst which tells them they're a *Gladiators* champion. For the disappointed runner-up, hitting the crash mat at least signals the end of the most gruelling physical examination they're ever likely to face.